A Walk on the

Wild Side

Important note

In this book you'll see children playing with animals. Some animals are friendly, but some are dangerous! NEVER approach or try to touch an animal in the wild unless a grown-up has said it's safe to do so.

A Walk on the
Wild Side

Join the adventure to see animals around the world

Louis Thomas

Frances Lincoln
Children's Books

I study animals lots. I want to become a proper studier of animals, which is called a zoologist. So last year I decided to go on an ADVENTURE. Taking this scrapbook and my friend Joe (that's him below, with the sticky-up hair), I traveled the world through jungles, across oceans, in the woods, on safari, and on farms. It was a bit dangerous, but I wasn't scared. I drew pictures of animals and wrote about the things they're good at, their families, and their homes, and put everything right here in this book.

This is my walk on the wild side!

CONTENTS

The BIG, WILD WORLD...

Desert, woodland, jungle, and grassland are all different animal homes, called habitats. They can be found in many places. Here are some of the ones we visited.

WOODLAND

JUNGLE

FARM

GRASSLAND

GRASSLAND

OCEAN AND ISLANDS

JUNGLE

Meet the
FARM
ANIMALS

On planet Earth, many animals are bred by humans, for their milk, eggs, or meat. Farms can be found all over the world, so we decided to visit a few on our journey. There was lots to see (and smell). We thought farms would be some of the safest places we'd go, but there were some hidden dangers, and we hadn't counted on this rooster . . .

This is Samuel, my favorite **PIG** in the whole world. Pigs are different colors and have different patterns depending on what breed they are.

Samuel spends his day rolling around in the mud. People say that pigs do this to keep cool, but I think it just makes Samuel happy.

This cow is a boy, which is called a **BULL**. We didn't get too close. Bulls like to use their horns to defend themselves against threats.

You can tell how old a cow is by the length of its horns. The longer the horns the older the cow.

The hair on a horse's head is called a mane.

Horse riding is quite difficult but luckily I'm very good at it. **HORSES** are ungulates, which means they have hooves. These are great for galloping.

People say that dogs and chickens can't talk, but I know better.

GOATS eat ALL THE TIME, even more than me and Joe. They'll keep on eating until there's nothing left, and they might not stop then!

Male goats butt heads with their horns to fight for power.

Did you know you can milk goats like you can cows? I like goat cheese.

In every group of **CHICKENS** there is a pecking order. One chicken is the boss at the top, and gets to eat and drink first, while one is last in line at the bottom. Even chicks that are only one week old have a pecking order!

It takes 21 days for chicks to grow inside eggs before they hatch.

Chicks take five to six weeks to grow all their feathers.

ROOSTERS are male chickens. They have long tail feathers, called sickle feathers, which they use to attract female chickens.

Cock-a-doodle-DOO!!!

In the morning, the head rooster (at the top of the pecking order) is the first to crow to announce the new day.

15

That's what you'll hear if you're in a field of fluffy **LAMBS** that are following you around. Lambs are young sheep. They eat a lot of grass so their stomachs have four chambers to help digestion.

This is a girl **COW** (not like the bull earlier). It still has horns to protect itself from danger, but it's less likely to charge you.

This goose wouldn't try sitting on a bull.

Cows' stomachs have four chambers like lambs.

On our journey we saw many creatures who lived in or around water, whether fresh (like lakes and rivers) or salty (in the ocean). Scuba gear let us explore this amazing watery world...

Meet the
OCEAN and ISLAND
ANIMALS

I soon realized that fish are incredible.
They come in different colors and
sizes, but most of them swim using
their fins. They have scales (bony
plates) on their bodies for protection.

The **ATLANTIC SAILFISH** uses its upper jaw like a spear, to slash into shoals of fish.

The spear of the sailfish we saw was three feet long!

21

Yes, that's right. Some fish can FLY. I didn't believe it either until I saw it with my own eyes. To get away from predators, **FLYING FISH** jump out of the water and let their winglike fins carry them on air currents.

Sharks are dangerous. Don't do what I'm doing in this picture (I made friends with this one first which is why it's OK).

HAMMERHEAD SHARKS get their name because of the shape of their head. The eyes at each end give them all-around vision.

BLUE WHALES are the largest living animals on the planet and can grow to nearly 100 feet long. They live in the ocean, but they aren't fish. They're mammals, like us, and have to come to the surface to breathe.

WOOOOOOOSH!

When whales breathe out, the steam in their breath turns into water.

The **LITTLE BITTERN** is related
to herons and egrets but is smaller,
only growing to 13 inches in length.
It's hard to spot but you might see
it in reeds by the water, waiting to
pounce on fish with its large beak.

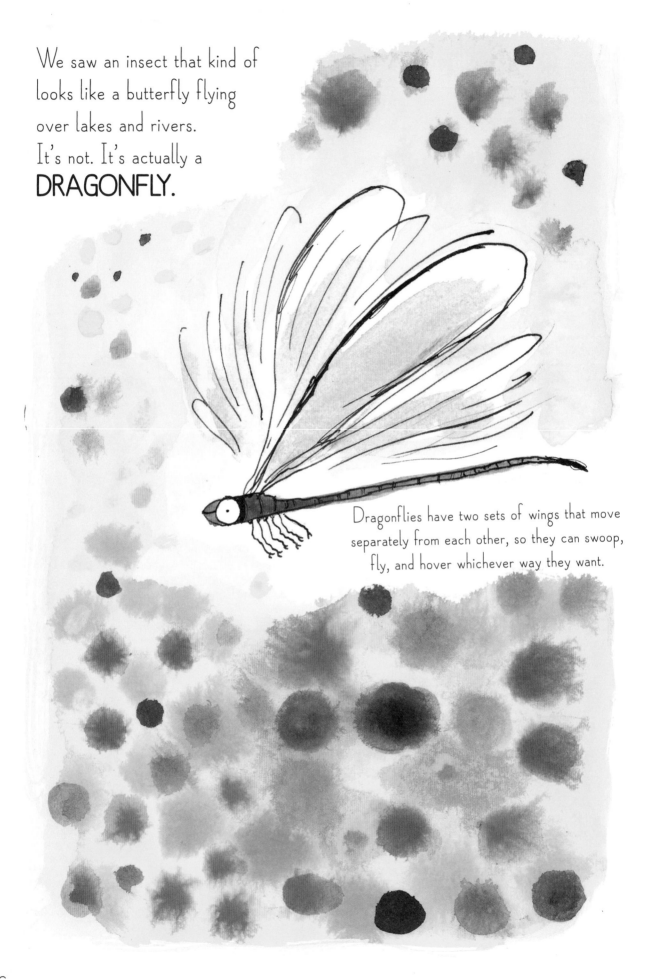

We saw an insect that kind of looks like a butterfly flying over lakes and rivers. It's not. It's actually a
DRAGONFLY.

Dragonflies have two sets of wings that move separately from each other, so they can swoop, fly, and hover whichever way they want.

PELICANS have a big throat pouch, which they use to scoop up large catches of fish (and children). Chicks reach into their parents' throats to gobble up fish that's already been partly digested.

Their webbed feet paddle through water when they're trying to catch prey.

CRABS are crustaceans, which means they have their skeleton on the outside of their body instead of inside like humans. They use their pincers to grab food or to defend themselves from attackers.

Imagine if you had to carry your home around on your back! That's what a **HERMIT CRAB** does. It lives in cast-off shells to protect its soft body.

This is a **GREAT EGRET,** which is a type of heron. Its neck is shaped like an S and is really bendy, which helps it to spear prey fast. Its long legs help it walk through wetland like marshes.

FROGS are amphibians – cold-blooded creatures that live in or near ponds, lakes, and rivers. They eat insects, but big frogs can even eat small lizards and mammals like mice. This frog is called Josephine.

The **GREEN TURTLE** is a tropical creature. It's one of the biggest sea turtles in the world. When it's not swimming thousands of miles across the ocean it likes sunbathing, like this!

Don't try to ride a turtle unless you're good friends.

HAWKSBILL TURTLES

have a pointed beak. They use this to dig out sponges from crevices to eat.

Meet the
JUNGLE ANIMALS

The jungle was the most
colorful place we visited on the planet.
Rain forests cover only six percent of the
earth, but they contain over half of its plant and
animal species. We were amazed at all the things we
spotted. We had to keep our eyes and ears alert, though, as
some of the animals weren't too friendly . . .

This **MACAW** is a kind of parrot. It's got nice bright colors and it's supersmart. By the end of the day, this one could copy every word we said, and we even taught him to wave, dance, and somersault off his branch.

We found this **RING-TAILED LEMUR** on the island of Madagascar, which is the only place in the world you can see it. It has large hands and feet, and moves around on all fours easily—like Joe!

Amazingly, **CROCODILES** don't sweat.
To keep cool, they open their mouths and
"mouth gape," which is a lot like panting.
It shows LOTS of teeth . . .

TOUCANS live in
the rain forest and use
their beaks to pluck
and peel fruit. They
also use their tongues
to catch insects, frogs,
and reptiles . . . and
talk to other birds.

HUMMINGBIRDS are teeny-tiny, sometimes only the size of your thumb. Some can beat their wings 80 times a second, making the humming noise that gives them their name.

These scary sticklike insects can turn their heads
180 degrees to look for ladybugs to eat for lunch!

Girl **PRAYING MANTISES** will
eat boys after mating with them.

ORANGUTAN means "person of the forest," as orangutans spend most of their time in trees. They swing from branches using their arms, which span over 6 feet wide from fingertip to fingertip when stretched out.

Orangutans, like most primates, enjoy grooming their children. If you're lucky you might get a head massage!

The largest snake in the Belize Jungle, the **BOA CONSTRICTOR** can reach an amazing length of 13 feet from head to tail. Sometimes it's hard to see where it begins and ends, or which end belongs to which head.

CHAMELEONS are very sneaky. Their eyes can move separately from each other, so they can look for their dinner in two different directions.

We saw this **LEOPARD** prowling through the grass when we were in the jungle. Leopards are so strong they can haul their prey up into trees when they've killed it. It's lucky we made friends with this one!

Most species of **GECKO** are nocturnal, which means they are active at night. To see better in the dark, they have a lens in each of their eyes that gets bigger in darkness, making their eyes much more sensitive to light than ours.

Like humans, the **GREEN IGUANA** is friendly and likes to be around others of its kind. Groups can be found searching for food in trees. These iguanas were drinking water from raindrops on flowers and leaves.

Meet the
DESERT and
GRASSLAND
ANIMALS

There are only two seasons in the grasslands: wet and dry, while deserts are areas with very little rainfall at all. Animals that live here have adapted to long periods where food and water are scarce. The best place to find animals in dry land is a waterhole. Once we realized this, we met some of the biggest friends ever . . .

HIPPOPOTAMUSES live in Africa, spending up to 16 hours a day keeping cool in shallow lakes and rivers. They leave at dusk to feed.

Hippos can grow to over 13 feet long. They're HUGE!

Why do **CAMELS** have humps? So that we can sit on them, of course. But the humps also store fat, which camels can use when there isn't much to eat. Camels live in the desert and can go for weeks without eating.

Adult male **LIONS** weigh nearly 450 pounds. They have sharp claws and teeth, as they have to defend their group (called a pride) from threats. This one was very friendly but it's really not a good idea to approach lions.

Only male lions have manes. Scientists think the length and color of a lion's mane is a signal to other lions about how good at fighting it is.

49

AFRICAN ELEPHANTS are the biggest land animals on earth. One elephant can eat up to 650 pounds of food every day and drink up to 50 gallons of water. But sometimes there's still enough water left for a water fight!

African elephants can grow to over 10 feet tall.

EGRETS sometimes like to get a free ride off an elephant, to save energy. Also, they can eat the insects kicked up when the elephant walks.

We saw this **TIGER** in grassland just outside a forest in India, and kept our distance. Tigers are the biggest cats of all. Adults can grow up to 10 feet long and are ferocious hunters.

They hunt animals like antelope and buffalo at night, lying in wait or stalking their prey until they're close enough to pounce. In the midday heat, though, they're more likely to be asleep.

Boy **GIRAFFES** can grow nearly 20 feet tall! Their long necks help them reach food.

Their black tufted tails swat away flies and other insects.

RHINOCEROSES are herbivores. Their big horns are used to fight other rhinos for territory.

MEERKATS live in burrows in "mobs" of around 50. When they're out looking for food, one meerkat will act as a lookout. If there's a threat, this meerkat will alert the others and everyone will run underground to safety.

In Africa I realized that no two **ZEBRAS** have the same pattern of stripes. Many scientists believe the reason zebras have stripes is to do with flies. Flies prefer to land on all-white or all-black surfaces rather than stripy ones, so by being stripy, zebras avoid being bitten and getting diseases.

Baby zebras are called foals. They stay close to their mothers and drink their milk for up to a year.

AFRICAN BUFFALO live in herds numbering up to a thousand. The way they eat is a bit gross. They swallow grass, then bring some of it back up to their mouth and chew this "cud" so they can absorb more of the nutrients.

It takes up to five years for the horns to grow.

Meet the
WOODLAND
ANIMALS

The woods were
the last stop on our
journey, but when we
entered, we knew the
danger wasn't over.
The tree canopy kept
the light out, and leaves
crackled under our feet,
telling everyone exactly where
we were! But luckily, there
were lots of friends to
be found . . .

These wide, branching antlers are only found on male **DEER**. They are very sharp and normally used to fight other males for territory.

Deer usually live in small herds for protection.

BROWN BEARS live in Asia, Northern Europe, and North America, so you might see one near you. But be careful! Bears can be dangerous.

They can keep warm in extreme cold because of their thick brown coats.

This **RACCOON** saw us before we saw it as raccoons have excellent night vision.

Their sense of smell is good too, so raccoons search for food with their noses on the ground, sniffing for insects, mice, birds, eggs, and plants. They're not fussy!

It's only male **PEAFOWL** that have this beautiful plumage, and they only have it to attract females during the breeding season (April to September). The more spots, the better chance they have of finding a mate.

OWLS are hunters of the night. They have big eyes that let in lots of light, allowing them to see in the dark. Their large rounded wings don't need to be flapped a lot, so they can swoop down silently on their prey.

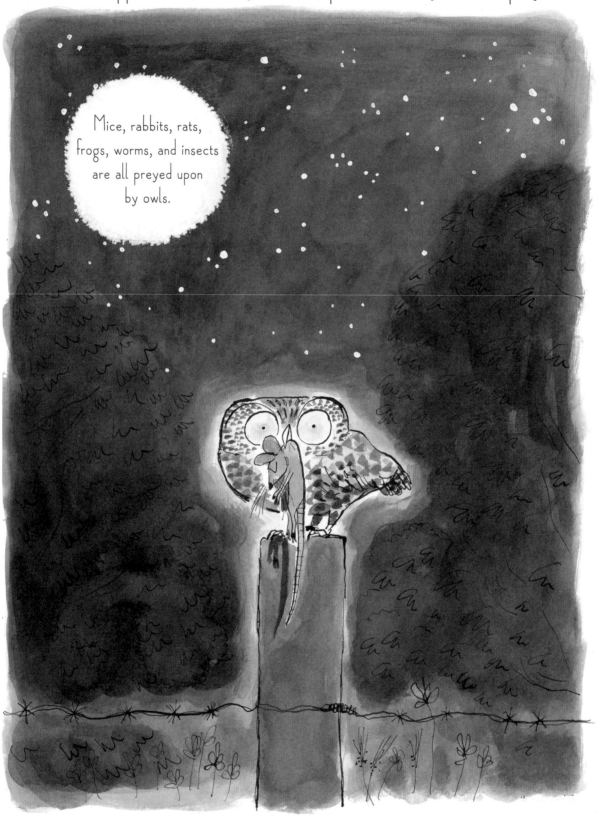

Mice, rabbits, rats, frogs, worms, and insects are all preyed upon by owls.

GRAY WOLVES howl loudly. It's their way of communicating with other members of their pack to decide when they're going to hunt. In each pack, there will be an alpha male who is the boss.

ANTEATERS don't have any teeth. To feed, they tear an opening in an anthill with their claws, then use their long tongue to flick up ants into their mouth, where they swallow them whole.

The **RED FOX** is one of the world's most common meat-eaters. It survives in many habitats because it eats lots of different things.

BATS are the only mammals that can fly, but they don't have feathers. Long arm, hand, and finger bones support a wing membrane instead.

You can see what type of bat this is by its fangs. It's a common **VAMPIRE BAT**, which means it sucks the blood of animals like horses and cows.

Meet the
ANIMALS
AT HOME

After our journey around the world, you'd think we'd
be sick of animals, right? Wrong! It was great to get
home and catch up with old friends. Sometimes we forget
what we can see on our own doorsteps, if we just look . . .

DOGS are closely related to foxes and wolves, and like them, many species can run really fast if they're hunting for prey. But some dogs, like my pet, Alfie, prefer to lie around in the sunshine.

If you look in your garden or a park near your house, you'll probably find a **MOUSE**. It scurries around to find nuts, seeds, and insects to eat, then goes back to its nest, which might be belowground or in someone's house.

The mouse is unlucky as it's food for lots of animals including owls, foxes, and wolves. But its big ears help it to hear predators coming.

Robbie is a **MACAW.** Like the one we saw in the wild, I can teach him to say lots of different things.

This is Priscilla, Joe's dog. She's a mongrel, which means she is a mixture of different breeds. But she has long legs and powerful muscles, so we're sure she's got some **GREYHOUND** in her.

Priscilla can run really fast for short periods of time, almost like a cheetah. Did you know that the fastest greyhounds can run over 50 feet per second?!

CATS are also popular pets for humans. Can you believe that these pets are related to lions and tigers? I couldn't, but then I looked at my cat Shabby's sharp claws and teeth . . .

Like tigers, many cats will hunt at night and be less active during the day, when it's hot. Here, Shabby is conserving his energy.

Domestic cats will hunt birds, mice, and anything small that they can catch. However, lots of them are used to being fed by humans. Look at my cat Veronique meowing for some fish!

GOLDFISH came from China and Central Asia, but now they can be found around the world. They are ray-finned fish so they have a hard skeleton, which gives them more control when swimming. That's why Gulpy can swim backward!

This **GREAT TIT** likes to come and drink in my fountain every day before flying back to the woods. Sometimes, I put out nuts and seeds, which it cracks open and eats. I've also seen it eating spiders and other insects.

Like all animals, I need my exercise. So does my pet **HAMSTER**, Bolt. He's 7 inches long and can run on his little legs for ages! If he's awake, that is. Hamsters normally sleep during the day.

Some people think **SPIDERS** are scary but many of them aren't dangerous to humans. They have organs called spinnerets that make silk threads, perfect for weaving sticky webs to catch prey that they kill with their venom.

So that's the story of my **WALK ON THE WILD SIDE**. Now that I'm back I can't wait to start planning my next adventure. Maybe I'll go to the Sahara desert to see ants that survive the hot sun by burrowing under the sand. Maybe I'll travel to the South Pole to see penguins. Or maybe I'll take a submarine down deep into the ocean, to say hello to creatures I've never even dreamed of. The world is a big place, and there's so much to see and so many animals to meet!

Where do **YOU** want to go?

FIND YOUR FAVORITE ANIMAL...

To Giovanna,
who made this trip possible, and therefore this book possible.
L.T.

First published in the USA in 2016 by Frances Lincoln Children's Books,
142 West 36th Street, Fourth Floor, New York, NY 10018, USA
QuartoKnows.com
Visit our blogs at QuartoKnows.com

ISBN 978-1-84780-914-8

Illustrated in watercolor

Commissioned by Rachel Williams • Production by Jenny Cundill and Kate Pimm
Written by Katie Cotton • Designed by Andrew Watson

Printed in China

1 3 5 7 9 8 6 4 2